WEB WISDOM

How to Buy and Share Files Safely Online

Alison Morretta

Cavendish Square
New York

Published in 2015 by Cavendish Square Publishing, LLC
243 5th Avenue, Suite 136, New York, NY 10016

Library of Congress Cataloging-in-Publication Data

Morretta, Alison.
How to buy and share files safely online / Alison Morretta.
pages cm. — (Web wisdom)
Includes bibliographical references and index.
ISBN 978-1-50260-189-6 (hardcover) ISBN 978-1-50260-188-9 (ebook)
1. Computer file sharing—Juvenile literature. I. Title.

QA76.9.F5M665 2015
006.7—dc23

2014019949

Editor: Andrew Coddington
Senior Copy Editor: Wendy A. Reynolds
Art Director: Jeffrey Talbot
Designer: Douglas Brooks
Senior Production Manager: Jennifer Ryder-Talbot
Production Editor: David McNamara
Photo Research by J8 Media

The photographs in this book are used permission and through the courtesy of: Cover photo by
Aaltazar/iStock Vectors/Getty Images; graphicnoi/iStock/Thinkstock, 4; Martina_L/iStock/Thinkstock, 7;
John G. Mabanglo/AFP/Getty Images, 9; Gabe Palacio/Getty Images Entertainment/Getty Images, 11; Ivan
Solis/E+/Getty Images, 14; Günay Mutlu/E+/Getty Images, 16; Bloomberg/Getty Images, 19; william87/
iStock Editorial/Thinkstock, 20; 360b/Shutterstock.com, 22; © iStockphoto.com/manaemedia, 24; Image
by Catherine MacBride/Moment Select/Getty Images, 25; Image Source RF/Sydney Bourne/Image
Source/Getty Images, 26; © iStockphoto.com/Ldf, 28; mediaphotos/Vetta/Getty Images, 30; Dimitri Otis/
Digital Vision/Getty Images, 31; © iStockphoto.com/hocus-focus, 32; Felipe Micaroni Lalli/File:Microsoft
Keyboard.jpg/Wikimedia Commons, 34; Ugurhan Betin/E+/Getty Images, 36; Boston Globe via Getty
Images, 38.

Contents

CHAPTER 1

File Sharing: Why It Matters

Every day, when you share photos or videos with friends and family, download and email schoolwork, or create your own art and music and share it with others, you are using file sharing technology. The Internet is also a fast and easy way to access content created by others, be it art, music, television, movies, or games. Buying and sharing files is a great way to share user-created content to gain an audience for your work. It also allows us to access the things we already like, and exposes us to new and different things we may not have known about otherwise.

For all the possibilities that buying and sharing files on the web opens up to us, there are many dangers as well. Many websites offer content that is under **copyright**, or owned by someone else, and sharing and downloading those files is a very serious crime. There are also many dangerous computer viruses hidden in files or pop-up ads that can seriously damage your computer and steal your personal information. It is important to identify and recognize these threats in order to use the Internet safely and legally to get and share the things you love with others.

Early File Sharing Technology

The first technology for creating a network, or link between computers, was developed in 1985, when the **FTP (File Transfer Protocol)** system was created. Back then it was used mostly by computer scientists and engineers, as the modern-day personal computer (PC) was not yet available to the public. The FTP system was very complex and required the user to know many commands in order to use it, but it was the first technology that allowed files to be transferred between users. FTP technology is still used by many people, but modern FTP servers are much faster and more user-friendly.

The earliest form of peer-to-peer (P2P) file sharing seems primitive today. Even though the personal computer became popular during the mid-1980s, the Internet as we know it had not been invented yet. In order to share files, people used floppy disks. These disks, which had 1.4 megabytes (MB) of memory, were inserted into a computer's disk drive, allowing the user to access or copy files, as well as save their own files to the disk. In order to share files, a person would have to physically give the disk to another person, who could then save the files to their own computer.

In the late 1980s and early 1990s computer games such as *Oregon Trail*, *Myst*, and *Where in the World is Carmen Sandiego?* became very popular. These games, which came on floppy disks (and later CD-ROM discs), were installed and playable on one computer. Some people started to copy and share these games using blank discs. In 1992, the first major anti-copyright infringement campaign, known as "Don't Copy That Floppy," was started by the Software Publishers Association (SPA) to educate the public that copying these games was illegal.

Before the Internet, people used floppy disks to copy and transfer files from one computer to another.

The World Wide Web

People have been using file sharing illegally for almost as long as the technology has been available, but the process became much quicker and easier after the development of the Internet. In 1989, British computer scientist Tim Berners-Lee invented the World Wide Web. Berners-Lee was inspired to invent the web while working as a software engineer at a physics laboratory near Geneva, Switzerland. He saw that the scientists there, who lived all over the world, found it difficult to share their data and results with one another after they had left the lab.

The World Wide Web became available to the general public in 1993. Since many people owned personal computers by the mid-1990s, Internet services such as America Online (AOL) and Yahoo!, which offered instant messaging and web browsing services, became incredibly popular. Email became an important form of communication, with free, web-based services such as Hotmail emerging. Also at this time, the first e-commerce sites, such as Amazon, allowed people to buy goods on the web. Anyone with access to a computer could now share files with anyone in the world.

The MP3 and Napster

A major event in the history of file sharing technology is the development of the MP3 file. The files could be created from compact discs, or CDs, and the resulting MP3 files saved onto a computer. The first portable MP3 players, which could store a lot more music, created an alternative to the portable CD player. Programs such as WinAmp turned the PC into a digital music library that could play anything available on the user's computer.

In 1999, teenagers Shawn Fanning and Sean Parker launched Napster, a file sharing site that would revolutionize the way the world listened to music. Napster was a program that made it possible for users to share the music on their hard drive with

Napster co-founder Sean Fanning ran into legal trouble when his popular website was ruled to be in violation of copyright laws.

other users anywhere in the world. Its user base grew rapidly through word of mouth. At its peak, Napster had over 70 million users. For the first time, people could access practically anything ever recorded with an Internet connection and a quick keyword search. This kind of access to the world's music, in addition to Napster's chat capabilities, made it possible to connect with other people who liked the same music as well as to expose people to music and bands they would not otherwise have known.

While a technological breakthrough and a music lover's dream, Napster ran into legal complications. When the United States Congress passed the Digital Millennium Copyright Act (DMCA) in 1998, it established copyright laws for content available on the Internet. By giving all its users free access to music that was under copyright, the record companies believed that Napster was violating the law. Although many artists supported Napster because it expanded their audience, some spoke out against the site. Both hip-hop artist Dr. Dre and the heavy metal band Metallica were very public in their opposition to Napster, and Metallica filed a lawsuit against the company in 2000 after a not-yet-released recording of their song "I Disappear" was leaked.

All the major record companies and members of the Recording Industry Association of America

(RIAA) pursued legal action against Napster in 2001, and the company was found guilty of copyright infringement. Napster filed for bankruptcy after paying hefty legal fees and fines, and the site was shut down. Though Napster itself failed, digital music had replaced audio CDs as the preferred media.

The Age of Digital Media

Portable MP3 players had been around since 1998, but when Apple founder Steve Jobs introduced the iPod in 2001, everything changed. The iPod was a small device with 5 gigabytes, or GB, of storage capacity that could hold 1,000 songs. The iTunes software program made it easy for Mac users to create a digital music library from their CDs. Apple introduced a PC-friendly version of the iPod the following year. The iTunes Music Store, introduced in 2003, took the Napster concept and added a

With the introduction of the iPod, Apple founder Steve Jobs revolutionized the way the world purchases and listens to music.

pay-per-download structure that satisfied artists and record companies. Within a few months, iTunes users had downloaded over 10 million songs, and that number more than doubled when iTunes was made available for Windows. Soon the iPod became the best-selling music device in history.

In 2005, the now-renamed iTunes Store expanded to include television shows and music videos, and full-length movies were available the following year. This concept of being able to watch movies and TV on demand, either on your computer or on a portable device, was revolutionary. Later Apple products, such as the iPhone and the iPad, were capable of playing music and video, as well as running various applications, such as Facebook, that could be downloaded from the iTunes Store.

Other companies, like the online book retailer Amazon, also began to offer music and video. They also introduced the Kindle, an e-book reader that made it easy for people to create a digital book library, and e-books have since started to replace traditional books. Amazon MP3 was launched in 2007, and Amazon Video On Demand (later renamed Amazon Instant Video) was launched in 2008. This service allows people to rent or buy television and movies. Other subscription-based online streaming video services, such as Netflix and Hulu, have become popular ways to watch television and movies on a variety of portable devices.

Illegal Downloads and Digital Piracy

Although there are many legal ways to acquire digital content on the Internet, many people continue to download files illegally through P2P networks. Though it seems harmless, this is a crime called **digital piracy**. It is also dangerous because many of these sites contain viruses that can seriously damage your computer and steal your personal information.

In 2001, the **BitTorrent** (or torrent) technology was introduced. It allowed users to download portions of files from different sources at the same time, which increased download speed. This was different from P2P sites like Napster, where the full file would come from a single source. The decentralized form of file sharing made it more difficult to trace, and many illegal download sites started using this technology to avoid legal trouble. The Pirate Bay, which originated in Sweden in 2003, has been shut down many times but continues to operate by moving its site around the world. Limewire was shut down in 2010, and the popular Megaupload site shut down in 2012. Despite the efforts by law enforcement to stop digital piracy, torrenting sites continue to thrive on the Internet.

CHAPTER 2

Buying and Sharing Basics

Before you buy, share, or download any files, you should take some safety precautions. Make sure that you have antivirus software installed, since many files on the Internet include **malware** and **spyware** that can "infect" your computer. Malware is a type of program, such as a virus, that damages or erases files on your computer. Spyware is a type of software that allows someone to secretly steal information from your computer's hard drive. These types of programs are embedded into many downloadable files, especially illegal downloads. Anti-virus and anti-spyware software protects your computer from these threats and keeps your computer and personal information safe.

Buying Files

Most commercially produced music, television shows, movies, and books are available electronically. The most commonly used paid digital download sites are the iTunes Store and Amazon. Buying files online requires you to register and supply your billing and credit card information, and you should never do this without first getting permission from your parents. It is important that they know how and where their credit cards are being used at all times. It is safe to provide credit card information on sites such as iTunes and Amazon because they store personal information securely by **encrypting** the data. Your browser will display a lock icon to verify that the site is safe to use, and the site's URL should start with "https:," which means that the file transfer is secure and encrypted.

The "lock" symbol and "https" URL protocol let users know that a site is secure and stores all user information safely.

The content you download from commercial sites is for personal use only. Since these files are under copyright protection, it is illegal to distribute them to others online. If you are unable to purchase files, there are a lot of safe, free options for listening to music and watching videos. Internet radio sites such as Pandora and Spotify allow you to stream music on your computer or mobile device. YouTube and Vimeo have billions of user-created videos to choose from, and Hulu offers movies and episodes of popular TV shows available to stream instantly.

Before You Share a File

If you have created your own digital content and want to share it online, there are several options from which to choose. However, before you share your work, you should decide how you want it to be used. Many people create content with the intention of sharing it so that others can change and build on what they have done. For example, using your music in a video, or sampling from that music to create your own. If you want to allow others to use your work, you should consider getting a free Creative Commons license.

Creative Commons

The Creative Commons organization was founded in 2001 to address the issue of copyright protection in the age of digital file sharing. When content is created, the original creator automatically holds the copyright to their work (know as **intellectual property**), but in today's world many people want to share their work with others. Artists, musicians, writers, and filmmakers may want to allow other people to use their work, or even allow them to build on it or reinvent it. Creative Commons offers free licensing to content creators so they can choose what kind of usage they want to allow, fostering a global community of shared creative wealth and collaboration.

Whatever kind of content you are creating, it is very simple to protect your work using Creative Commons. All CC licenses require attribution (giving credit to the creator of the original work). No matter what online platform you are using, it is important to always identify the author of the work you are sharing or using. You wouldn't want someone passing your hard work off as their own, so always give credit to the creator of the things you share online.

If you want to protect and share your own digital content, you can get a free license on the

Creative Commons website (creativecommons.org) and make it easy for people to credit you and use your work the way you want it used. There are different types of licenses available, so you can choose the one that is right for the intended purpose of your creation. You can choose to give people the right to tweak, remix, or reinvent your work, or allow people to share it only in its full, original form. You can allow people to use your work commercially or restrict it to noncommercial use. You can make sure that the person using your work shares any **derivative** works with others using the same license, or allow them to license it however

Despite many attempts by authorities to shut it down, The Pirate Bay remains one of the most frequently used torrenting sites for illegal file sharing and downloading.

they choose. Whatever type of license you pick, you will always be credited for the original work.

If you are looking for content to use, Creative Commons gives you the ability to search sites like YouTube, Flickr, SoundCloud, and Wikimedia for content that is licensed for use. Always check the type of license before using any content, and make sure that you respect the terms when adapting it and sharing it online, including providing the correct credit information and, when possible, a link to the original source.

Sharing Photos

Whether you are sharing personal photos with friends and family or pursuing photography as a

Flickr is a popular photo sharing website where both amateur and professional photographers can share their work with others.

hobby or potential career, sharing your pictures online is a great way to connect with others. Flickr is one of the largest photo sharing sites on the Internet and enables you to share both personal and artistic photos. The site gives you the option of making your photos public or private. To use Flickr, you have to register for a free account through Yahoo!, which owns the site. Once you have registered, you can upload photos from your desktop, or from mobile devices using the Flickr app. Before you upload any photos, you should adjust your account settings to reflect what information you want visible, who can view your photos, and how you want your photos shared. Flickr is also a great resource for discovering other artists, and easily allows you to share their work with your friends through social media sites like Facebook and Tumblr.

Sharing Music

Whether you are a musician looking for a larger fanbase or just want to share some of your tracks with friends and family, SoundCloud is a great choice for sharing your files online. This site requires you to register for an account, and the basic service is free. You can adjust your account settings to reflect the way you intend to use the site and control what information others can view.

If you want to limit who can listen to your music, you can make your track private in the "Settings" tab after you upload it. This will give you a permalink, which you can then send to specific people. Private tracks do not appear on your public profile or come up in searches. If you are a musician looking to expand your audience, the "Advanced Profile" tab allows you to link your SoundCloud account to other social media sites and gain more exposure for your creations.

In addition to the ability to upload your own music, SoundCloud lets you create and share playlists, and stream music and playlists uploaded by others.

SoundCloud allows both aspiring and established artists to share their music and reach a larger audience.

It also provides a link for songs that are available for download. To protect artists, SoundCloud has a built-in feature that prevents you from uploading songs under copyright, even if you do not share them publically. If you upload a song that does not belong to you, SoundCloud can identify that material as copyright-protected. It will automatically remove it from your profile, and send you a message warning you of copyright infringement.

Sharing Videos

YouTube is the most popular and commonly used video sharing site in the world. You can watch videos for free without an account, and upload your own after you register. You should always make sure that you own the content you are uploading, and that any non-original work you have incorporated into your creation is licensed for use by others. Licensing information for other people's videos can be found at the bottom of the "About" section under the video. While you cannot download videos directly from YouTube, if the license allows use by others you can use a YouTube Downloader program to access the video file.

If you are unsure whether the video is licensed for use outside of YouTube, you can send a message to the user who uploaded it by clicking on their username. In their YouTube profile, there is an option to send them a message, and you can directly ask them for permission to use their video. Always use common sense when sharing content from YouTube, since some users upload content illegally. If the video contains commercially produced music or video, it is most likely violating copyright laws and should not be downloaded or shared.

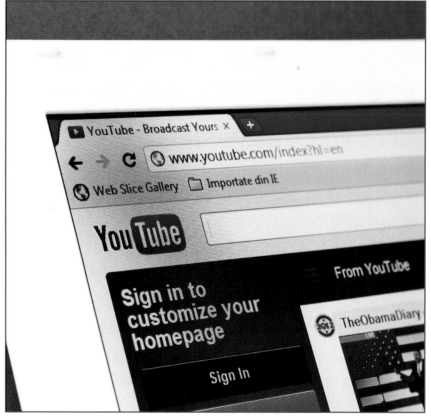

With more than one billion unique users visiting the site every month, YouTube is the most popular video sharing website in the world.

PHOTO SHARING SAFETY

When sharing personal photos on any form of social media, it is important to stay safe. As a general rule, you should always ask yourself, "Would I want my family or my teachers to see this photo?" If not, don't post it online. Once you post something on the Internet, there is no way to take it back, and if you post an inappropriate photo it can have very serious consequences. College admissions and employers use the Internet to search for information on applicants, and you can be rejected if they don't like what they find.

Unfortunately, even if your photo is appropriate for sharing, there are many **online predators** that use people's photos to obtain information about them. When you use your mobile phone to take pictures, the phone uses a process called **geotagging** to automatically store data on exactly where and when the photo was taken. It then embeds that data into the photo file so that when you share it, other people can access it. You can disable this feature on your phone, and you should do so if you plan on sharing personal photos online. If you don't, any stranger can find out specific details about you, including exactly where you live, where you go to school, and where you hang out with your friends.

CHAPTER 3

How Do You Do It Better?

Most file sharing sites have features for advanced usage that foster creative communities and exchanges between people who share the same interests. The ability to create customized playlists and photostreams, follow other users, leave feedback in comments sections, and "like" and share files on social media can enhance your file sharing experience.

Advanced Flickr Features

If you want to share birthday party, graduation, or other personal photos with a select group of people, you can use Flickr's "Groups" feature. This option allows you to create a group for family and friends that can only be accessed and viewed with an invitation from you. When you upload these photos, make sure to check the box that says "Private" so that they are only visible to you until you choose to share them. Flickr's **tagging** feature enables you to add descriptive labels to each of your photos. If you have made your photos public, adding tags helps other people find your work. You should include as much information about your public work as possible so that it is more likely to come up in a search. If you like someone's photo, be sure to "favorite" it and leave a comment on it. Positive feedback will always put a smile on the creator's face. Exploring tags for subjects you are

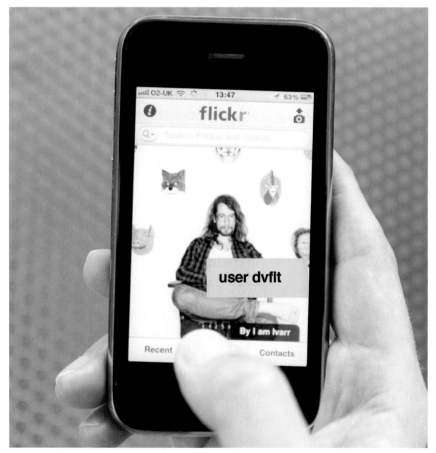

Whether on your computer or your mobile device, Flickr allows you to connect with other users and show your appreciation for their work.

interested in also helps you connect with other users by "following" them and to find groups on those topics. Whenever you join a group on Flickr, make sure you follow the uploading and posting rules outlined by the group's administrator.

Making the Most of SoundCloud

To get more out of SoundCloud, you should provide as much information about your track as possible. Give your track a title, provide a description, and use the tagging feature to identify the categories into which your track falls. If you have art you would like to accompany the track, upload it. The more information you give, the easier it will be for others to discover your music and the more likely they will be to listen to it. You should also make sure that you include the licensing information for your music when you upload it so that listeners know whether they can use your tracks in their own work.

Another important feature for sharing on SoundCloud is the ability to follow other users and comment on their tracks. SoundCloud displays music in waveform, and users can comment at specific points during the song. This means that if you hear a particularly great solo, you can comment at the exact time during the song and let the artists know how much you liked it. This feature is also great for giving feedback—if you think the artist can improve on something or the sound seems off to you, you can let them know where. You should always keep your comments constructive and helpful. SoundCloud is an interactive community for music lovers, and many of its users welcome collaboration and feedback to make their work better.

Commenting on the tracks of others is a great way to gain followers for your own music, since they are more likely to check out your profile if you "favorite" and "comment" on their music. It is considered spamming to directly ask other artists to listen to your music, either in comments or in messages, so you should not do that unless you

File sharing websites are a great way to discover new artists, expose your friends to new things, and collaborate on creative projects.

know the user personally. If you are interested in working with another artist, you can send them a message, and if they are interested in collaborating you can use the private sharing feature for your work-in-progress.

Using YouTube Better

YouTube has many advanced features that can improve your video sharing experience and help maintain your privacy. Even though the default setting for videos is public, you can also keep your videos private and share them only with select users. Keep in mind that you should never upload a video that you would not want your parents to see.

It is important to know your intended audience when you share things online. Make sure your privacy settings are set up properly before you post anything.

Even if your video is set to private, the people you share it with can easily show it to someone else.

To keep a video private, you will need to change it from public to private in the "Privacy Settings" section while it is uploading. If you want to change the setting after you have already uploaded your video, you can do so in the "Video Manager" section.

YouTube apps for mobile devices enable you to access all the site's content, no matter where you are.

You can use the "Unlisted" option to share with people that do not have a Google account, but when a video is unlisted, it is accessed through a link and anyone with the link can see it and add it to a playlist, which could be public. Private and unlisted videos do not appear on your public profile and do not come up in searches.

You can also create your own public channel, to which other users can subscribe. While your video is uploading, you can go to the "Advanced Settings" tab. Here you can allow users to rate and comment on your video and set the licensing information so that people know whether they can use your work. In the "Basic Info" tab, you can name your video, add a description for the viewer, and assign tags to help people find your work through keyword searches.

To get the most out of YouTube, you should browse to find channels that post videos relevant to your interests. Some of your favorite musicians, entertainers, and sports organizations may have their own YouTube channels you can subscribe to for all the latest content. YouTube also has dedicated pages for movies (youtube.com/movies) and TV shows (youtube.com/shows), some of which you can watch for free and some you can pay for and stream on demand. Always ask a parent before making an online purchase.

NETIQUETTE

The Internet has become such a huge part of people's lives that it is almost a world of its own, and all users have a responsibility to be good digital citizens. People share photos, videos, and other projects with others because they are excited about their creations, and the online communities created by file sharing should remain positive places for self-expression.

Because so many interactions on the Internet are anonymous, people sometimes act in ways they would not act in "real" life. However, it is important to always follow "netiquette" rules when online. Following these simple rules will make file sharing a positive experience and keep you safe at the same time.

- **Stay calm.** You should avoid using all capital letters when communicating with others online. Typing in all caps is seen as shouting and can offend people.

- **Keep your cool.** You should never send a message or post a comment when you are upset or angry. If you get an unkind comment, do not respond with an equally nasty message. If you feel threatened by anything someone says to you online, always tell a parent or teacher.

- **Be nice.** You should never say mean things about other people online, and this extends to the things they choose to share on the Internet. Being mean to others online is the same as being mean to their face, and **cyberbullying** can get you in serious trouble at home and at school.

- **Don't steal.** When people share things they have created, it is important to respect their hard work and creativity. Taking credit for their work or using it as your own is **plagiarism**. It is OK to share other people's work as long as you give them the proper credit and make sure you are not violating copyright laws.

- **Be clear.** Always use proper spelling and grammar when posting online so that other people can understand you.

- **Stay safe.** Never share private information, such as your full name, address, credit card information, and so on, on websites that are not verified as secure. Make sure you don't use identifying information in your screen names or in chat rooms. When sharing personal photos, make sure that they are only accessible to family and close friends.

CHAPTER 4

Case Studies

While file sharing can help people to learn new things and share their creativity with others, there are consequences when it is done incorrectly or illegally. It is useful to examine some real-life stories about people's experiences with file sharing to put these benefits and risks in perspective.

Paying the Price for Piracy

Skyler Atterbom, a seventeen-year-old boy from Albuquerque, New Mexico, learned the hard way that the punishment for downloading copyrighted material is severe. Skyler used the website BitTorrent to download an illegal copy of the critically acclaimed film *The Hurt Locker* (2008). Though the film won the Oscar for Best Picture in 2009, it did not make much money at the box office, and the film's producers, Voltage Pictures, decided to file a digital piracy lawsuit against almost 25,000

BitTorrent users who had downloaded and shared their movie.

Like many kids his age, Skyler and his friends often downloaded movies and music from the Internet without really thinking that what they were doing was illegal. He got a wake-up call when the authorities traced the IP address for the computer he used to download the movie through his Internet service provider. They contacted Skyler's father, whose name was on the account, and ordered him to pay a $2,900 fine. Skyler's dad made him pay the fine himself, and he had to work all through that summer to pay back the money he

College student Joel Tenenbaum was sued by a group of major record companies for illegal downloading and file sharing. He was found guilty of violating copyright law and ordered to pay a $675,000 fine.

had borrowed from his family. Looking back on it, Skyler regrets that he did not just rent the film. He ended up paying almost $3,000 for a movie that he could have watched for one dollar.

Dangerous Downloads

Even if you don't get in legal trouble for illegal downloads, you can cause a lot of problems for yourself and your family. A thirteen-year-old girl from Connecticut learned this when she illegally downloaded an episode of her favorite TV show from a torrenting website. She missed the episode after getting home late from her soccer game and she didn't want to have it spoiled for her at school the next day. She knew it was illegal, but she thought that since she always watched the show on TV and it was only one time, it was okay. The file she downloaded was infected with malware, which damaged her computer and stole her parents' credit card information.

Her laptop started running very slow and her applications would quit unexpectedly, sometimes when she was in the middle of her homework and hadn't saved her progress. Soon her parents began to see several charges on their card statement that they had not made, and they confronted their daughter about using the credit card without permission. She had not made those purchases, but she told her parents that she thought she might have a computer virus from the file she had downloaded. The one file she downloaded cost her parents a lot of trouble and money. They spent a long time dealing with their credit card company and disputing the charges. It also cost them more than $300 to diagnose and repair her laptop. She had most of her laptop and credit card privileges taken away until she could afford to pay her parents back.

Learning Through Sharing

Not everyone learns the same way, especially when it comes to learning a new language. Some people are better at memorizing vocabulary words through written exercises and flash cards, and some people are better at learning by listening. This was the case for a student in a sixth-grade Spanish class in New York. He was having a lot of trouble with his verb tenses and his pronunciation, and he did not like to speak in class because he was embarrassed. He talked to his teacher about it, and she decided to make use of file sharing technology to help him improve his Spanish-speaking skills

Using SoundCloud's private sharing feature, the student was able to record himself speaking and send that file to his teacher. She could then listen to his exercises and insert comments at the exact time that something needed correction. She also recorded the correct versions and shared those with her student, who was able to keep that file so that he could listen to it as many times as he wanted. It did not take long for his verbal skills to improve and his grades to go up, and he was no longer embarrassed to speak in front of his class.

File sharing technology allows us to share the things we create with others and fosters a type of creativity and collaboration that would not have been possible before the digital age. However, with these technological advances comes the responsibility of being a good digital citizen. The Internet provides us with instant access to the world's media content, and with the ease of downloading and sharing files, it can be tempting to use this technology in the wrong way. While illegal downloading and sharing may seem like a harmless crime, it is not. The creators of the stolen work are the victims. You can also become the victim of a computer virus or other cybercrime if you download an infected file. With so many different ways to download and share files safely and legally, there is no excuse for stealing, and the risks are far greater than the benefits.

GLOSSARY

BitTorrent A peer-to-peer (P2P) file transfer protocol for sharing large amounts of data over the Internet, in which each part of a file downloaded by a user is transferred to other users; also called a torrent.

copyright The exclusive legal right to reproduce, publish, sell, or distribute the matter and form of something (as a literary, musical, or artistic work).

cyberbullying The use of cell phones, instant messaging, email, chat rooms, or social media to harass, intimidate, or threaten someone.

derivative Something (such as a creative work) that is based on another source or sources.

digital piracy The illegal trade in software, videos, digital video devices, and music that occurs when someone other than the copyright holder copies the product and distributes it.

encrypting Converting information or data into a cipher or code, especially to prevent unauthorized access.

FTP (File Transfer Protocol) A system for sending files from one computer to another computer over the Internet.

geotagging The addition of geographical information, usually in the form of latitude and longitude coordinates, to images, videos, and other types of digital data files.

intellectual property Something (such as an idea, invention, or creation) that comes from a person's mind.

malware Software that is intended to damage or disable computers and computer systems.

online predator A person who uses the Internet to commit crimes.

plagiarism Taking someone else's work or ideas and passing them off as one's own.

spyware Software that enables a user to obtain private information about another's computer activities by secretly transmitting data from their hard drive.

tagging Using keywords called tags to add descriptive information about online content so it can be categorized and searched.

FIND OUT MORE

The following books and websites will take you on the next step in your file sharing journey.

Books:

Levine, John R., and Margaret Levine Young. *The Internet for Dummies*. Hoboken, NJ: John Wiley & Sons, 2012.

Sechler, Jeff. *Internet Safety for Kids and Young Adults*. State College, PA: Privately published, 2012.

Suen, Anastastia. *Downloading and Online Shopping Safety and Privacy*. 21st Century Safety and Privacy. New York, NY: Rosen Publishing Group, 2013.

Websites:

Creative Commons
creativecommons.org

This official website provides updates, frequently asked questions, and step-by-step information on using and applying the Creative Commons licenses to your work.

Digizen for Kids
www.digizen.org/kids

This website provides educators, parents, and kids with specific advice and resources on issues such as social networking, cyberbullying, and digital citizenship.

NetSmartz Workshop
www.netsmartz.org/Teens

NetSmartz Workshop is an interactive, educational program of the National Center for Missing & Exploited Children that provides resources to help educate, engage, and empower children to be safer on- and offline.

BIBLIOGRAPHY

Fisk, Nathan W. *Cybersafety: Digital Piracy*. New York, NY: Chelsea House, 2011.

Fisk, Nathan W. *Understanding Online Piracy: The Truth About Illegal File Sharing*. Westport, CT: Praeger Publishers, 2009.

Ivester, Matt. *lol…OMG!: What Every Student Needs to Know About Online Reputation Management, Digital Citizenship, and Cyberbullying*. High School Edition. Reno, NV: Serra Knight Publishing, 2012.

Levine, John R., and Margaret Levine Young. *The Internet for Dummies*. Hoboken, NJ: John Wiley & Sons, 2012.

O'Keeffe, Gwen Schurgen. *Cybersafe: Protecting and Empowering Kids in the Digital World of Texting, Gaming, and Social Media*. Elk Grove Village, IL: American Academy of Pediatrics, 2010.

Sechler, Jeff. *Internet Safety for Kids and Young Adults*. State College, PA: CreateSpace, 2012.

Suen, Anastastia. *Downloading and Online Shopping Safety and Privacy*. 21st Century Safety and Privacy. New York, NY: Rosen Publishing Group, 2013.

Willard, Nancy E. *Cyber-Safe Kids, Cyber-Savvy Teens: Helping Young People Learn How to Use the Internet Safely and Responsibly*. San Francisco, CA: Jossey-Bass, 2007.

INDEX

ABOUT THE AUTHOR

Alison Morretta holds a Bachelor of Arts in English and Creative Writing from Kenyon College in Gambier, Ohio. She has worked in book publishing since 2005, developing and copy editing both fiction and nonfiction manuscripts. Alison is a writer and blogger and has written a number of nonfiction books for young adults, including another title in the Web Wisdom series, *How to Maintain Your Privacy Online*. She lives in New York City with her loving husband, Bart, and their rambunctious Corgi, Cassidy.